NATIONAL
MARITIME MUSEUM
GREENWICH

SPOTLIGHT SERIES

The *Princess Alice* Disaster

Tragedy on the Thames

Hannah Stockton

Contents

Introduction

Moonlight Trip

The ticket overleaf, numbered 7514 for the London Steamboat Company Limited 'Moonlight Trip to Rosherville & Back', permitted the holder to board one of the passenger paddle steamers heading down the River Thames for a day trip on 3 September 1878 (fig. 1). On its own, this piece of pasteboard is unassuming, a piece of historical scrap. However, the small

The ticket tells us that the return fare was two shillings, that it was only valid for the day it was issued, likely at Old Swan Pier, near London Bridge, and that it should be given up when the passenger returned from Rosherville Gardens, near Gravesend in Kent, that evening. In relatively good condition, the ticket has not been smudged, folded or torn – it does not bear the expected marks of a fun day out on the Thames.

Below the ticket itself is a small piece of wood, carved in the shape of a boat, accompanied by the label: 'carved from wood taken from Wreck of Steamer "Princess Alice". 1878'. In a different hand, a note explains that 'Pa decided not to go on trip after he had bought ticket'. It seems that 'Pa' and his descendants went to the effort to retrieve and carve this wood from the wreck and construct and label the display card to preserve it. What is clear is that the family attached emotional meaning to the ticket and to the historical significance of the event it marked.

This is far from a souvenir of a day trip on the Thames, it is a unique reminder of the sinking of *Princess Alice*. On 3 September 1878, the paddle steamer, returning more than 800 day trippers from the Kent coast to London, collided with a large cargo vessel, *Bywell Castle*, just off Woolwich. *Princess Alice* sank within minutes. It is still the worst disaster on an inland waterway in British history, resulting in more than 600 deaths and leaving countless others affected in its aftermath.

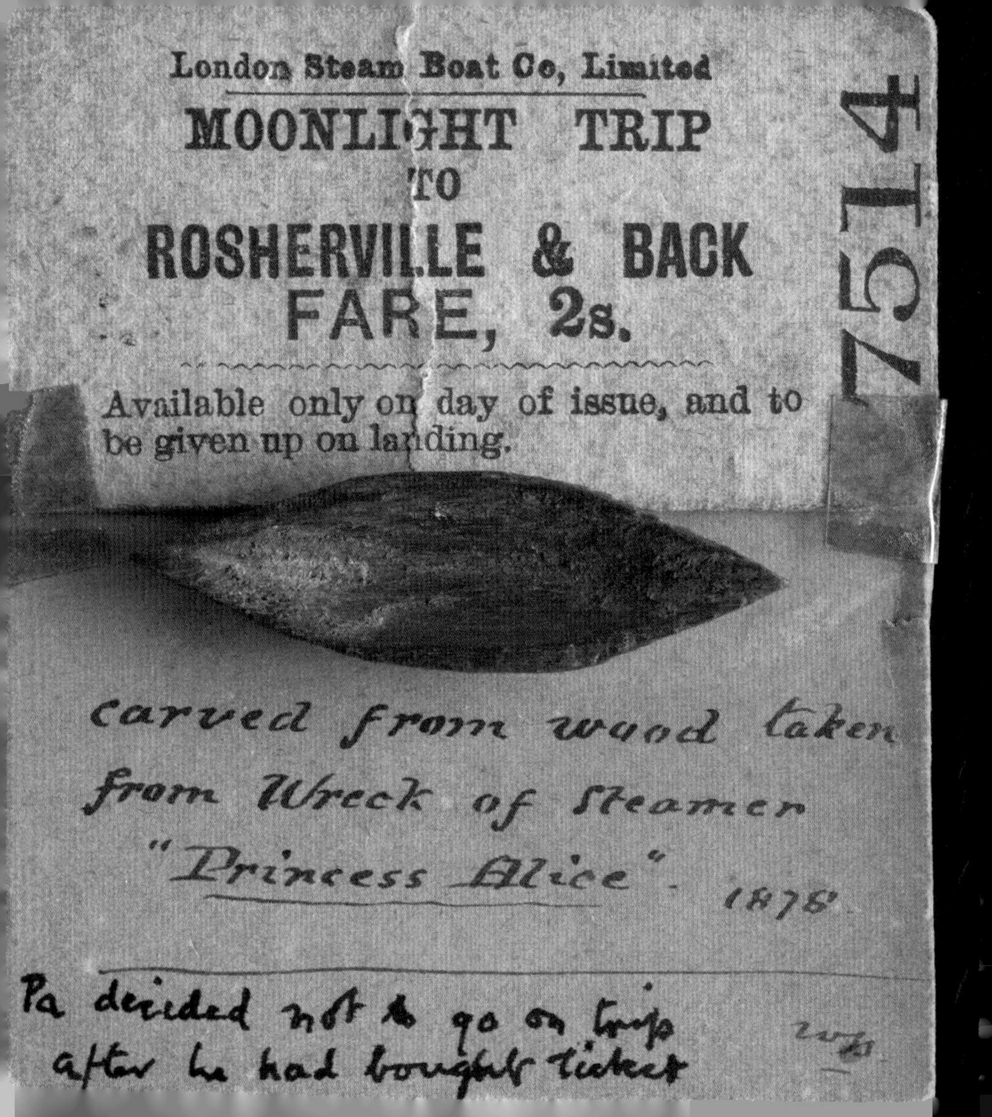
London Steam Boat Co, Limited
MOONLIGHT TRIP
TO
ROSHERVILLE & BACK
FARE, 2s.
Available only on day of issue, and to be given up on landing.
4157
carved from wood taken from Wreck of Steamer "Princess Alice". 1878
Pa decided not to go on trip after he had bought ticket

This memento, in both its making and preservation, marks the enduring impact on one particular family. Pa and his descendants, whoever they were, told their family story of chance and survival through this object, a family which might not have existed but for this unused ticket. Through Pa's ticket and carving we can trace the impact of the *Princess Alice* sinking on wider Victorian Britain – identifying how people mourned and came to terms with loss on this scale, how society adapted in response and how the memory of the *Princess Alice* disaster continues to be preserved.

FIG. 1 Excursion ticket for a 'Moonlight Trip to Rosherville & Back', unknown maker, 1878, 29 × 57 mm, REL0301

Chapter 1

'The place to spend a happy day'

The morning of 3 September 1878 promised to be the start of a beautiful day. Many *Princess Alice* passengers later reported that they had been inspired by the good weather to take a day trip down the river to seaside resorts at Gravesend, or onwards to the coast at Sheerness or Southend. The *Morning Advertiser* reported 'the fine weather tempting aboard many excursionists on the holiday trip' and *Princess Alice* passenger William Bishop later told a *Daily Chronicle* correspondent that he had remarked to a fellow passenger, 'the beautiful morning has done good for the boat company today'. Indeed, the day was so fine that the families of both Captain William Grinsted (1831–78), master of *Princess Alice*, and William Towse (1839–85), superintendent of the steamboat company, were on trips that day.

Nothing is known about the identity of Pa, who bought this ticket. Museum records show that it was donated by the daughter of William Baddeley (1848–1939) but, apart from what appear to be initials in the bottom right-hand corner, there is no indication whether the ticket belonged to him or was instead part of his collection of maritime curios. Pa's identity is likely lost to history, perhaps in part thanks to what turned out to be his lucky escape. It is possible that Pa, like William Bishop, was inspired to take his business trip by river to enjoy the fine weather, or he might simply have wanted to escape the city for a day.

The outward leg of these trips usually began at Old Swan Pier, near London Bridge, where half-hourly boats carried commuters and leisure travellers downriver in summer (fig. 2). The journey usually took around two hours, stopping at piers including Greenwich, Blackwall and North Woolwich, so that passengers could board anywhere along the route (fig. 3). The ticket does not name a specific vessel, and passengers could use whichever London Steamboat Company boat was available at the time. Therefore, we cannot know whether Pa would have been on board *Princess Alice*, even if he had used his ticket that day. Nor do we know at what point he changed his mind – did he travel down to Rosherville but take an earlier vessel back, or did he decide not to go at all and remain in London?

FIG. 2
Paddle steamer at Old Swan Pier, London Bridge, unknown photographer, about 1896, photograph, N44389

NE are appointed to sail from
or ten days, carrying goods at
rts of France and SWITZER-
cabin, 30s.; steerage, 15s.
N, Glasgow and Havre; or to
., Swansea.

CH SEA, BALTIC, &c.

INENTAL STEAM
E.—The GENERAL STEAM
ANY'S STEAMSHIPS leave
ear the Tower, for
aturday, and Sunday:—August
ne; 24th, at Ten; and 25th, at
5s.; fore cabin, £1 9s. Return
2 4s. Brokers, F. Stahlschmidt

24th, at Two Afternoon. Single
0s.

sday, and Saturday, at Noon.
16s. Return tickets:—Saloon,
, Weatherley, Mead, and Co.
:—August 21st, at Five After-
res:—Saloon, 18s.; fore cabin,
1.; fore cabin, £1 1s. Brokers,

, at Four; 21st, at Five; 22d, at
at Eight Afternoon. Fares:—
urn tickets:—Saloon, 18s. 6d;
Co.
ust 22d, at Eight Morning.
eturn tickets:—Saloon, 20s. 6d.;
ender, and Co.
August 21st, at Four After-
cabin, £2. Return tickets,
in, £5; fore cabin, £3 6s. 8d.
new steamships Kestrel and
ommodation, consisting of a
adies' cabin, and a comfortable
is station.
free of charge to and from the
are included in the fares.
rvice see bills, or apply to the
d, or at the Chief Offices, 71,
, Piccadilly, London.
ing and delivery business in
e loaded in or discharged from
including all charges, between
For particulars apply to the

TERSBURG TOWN.
m-house Quay.
F STEAMERS.
re:—
....Thursday, August 22.
llow weekly.

M,
, Mark-lane, London;
nd 38, Quay Side, Newcastle.

COPENHAGEN and

(Sundays excepted), at 11 A.M., calling at Blackwall and Tilbury Piers. Returning from Ramsgate daily (Sundays excepted), at 11 A.M., and Margate about Noon, until further notice. Single fares: Saloon, 5s.; fore cabin, 4s; children under 12 years of age, 2s. 6d. Perambulators free.

MARGATE and BACK, every Sunday, at 8.30, by the EAGLE.

For full particulars of through service see bills, or apply to the Company's Agents at the towns named; or at the Chief Offices, 71, Lombard-street, and 37, Regent-circus, Piccadilly, London.

The Company undertake all shipping and delivery business in London in connection with goods to be loaded in or discharged from their vessels, and make through rates, including all charges, between all ports to which the vessels trade. For particulars apply to the Secretary.

LONDON STEAMBOAT COMPANY (Limited).—IPSWICH, HARWICH, WALTON-ON-THE-NAZE, and CLACTON-ON-SEA.—The Steamer QUEEN OF THE THAMES or ORWELL will leave LONDON-BRIDGE at 9 30, call ng at Blackwall about 10, Woolwich 10 20, Tilbury about 11 15, daily, except Sundays.

UP-RIVER DAILY EXCURSIONS.

PUTNEY, HAMMERSMITH, and KEW, by STEAMBOATS—From CHELSEA at 11 A.M. till 6 P.M. at frequent intervals. Last Boat from Kew to the City about 8 P.M. For Hampton Court and Richmond, Sundays and Mondays, from London-bridge at 10 A.M.

ROSHERVILLE GARDENS and GRAVESEND.—DAILY, by commodious Steamers from LONDON-BRIDGE at 9 30, 10 0, 10 30, 11 0, 12 0, and 3 0. Also for SOUTHEND at 9 30 and 11, and for SHEERNESS at 9 30, 10 30, and 11, calling at BLACKWALL and NORTH WOOLWICH about half an hour after above-mentioned times. Fore cabin—Return, Gravesend, 1s. 6d.; Southend or Sheerness, 2s. 6d.—Special arrangements Bank Holiday.

MOONLIGHT TRIPS on the THAMES—GRAVESEND and back—Every Monday, Wednesday, and Saturday during the season, from London-bridge at 6 0; Greenwich, 6 30; and North Woolwich, 6 45.

EDINBURGH.—The magnificent Steamships MARMION, IONA, or MORNA, now leave HERMITAGE STEAM WHARF, Wapping, for LEITH, every Wednesday and Saturday. Fares (including Steward's fee): Saloon, 22s.; fore cabin, 16s.; state rooms for families, 32s. each berth. Deck (soldiers and sailors), 10s. Return tickets for one month, 34s. and 24s. 6d. Apply at G. W. Wheatley and Co.'s, 23, Regent-street, W.; Lavington's, 69, Old Bailey; or at the Wharf to
J. A. CLINKSKILL.

STEAM to BERWICK-ON-TWEED.—The LONDON AND EDINBURGH SHIPPING COMPANY'S fast S.S. ALBION will sail from Hermitage Steam Wharf every Saturday at 2 P.M. RETURNING from BERWICK every Wednesday. Return tickets, 30s. For particulars apply at the Wharf to J. A. CLINKSKILL.

SAILING SHIPS FOR AUSTRALIA, &c.

MESSRS. MONEY WIGRAM and SONS' LINE of STEAM and SAILING SHIPS for AUSTRALIA.—For MELBOURNE (Port Phillip) direct.—To leave the South West India Docks (where she is now lying for inspection) on Tuesday, August 20, calling at PLYMOUTH.—The splendid Clipper Ship ESSEX, 1,100 tons register, Robert Ticehurst, Commander. Her accommodation for all classes of passengers is unsurpassed, and the saloon cabins are fitted with cabin furniture.

FIG. 3
London Steamboat Company advertisement from the *Shipping and Mercantile Gazette*, 19 August 1878

'An endless vista of masts'

The middle of the nineteenth century was a time of rapid change for transport in the city. The Thames had long been London's main highway, necessary in a city with few bridges and poor-quality roads. Even in the mid-1800s, when its passenger and cargo trade was threatened by the rapid expansion of railway lines across the country, the river was an 'endless vista of masts [...] used to bring and diffuse the riches of every part of the world over this little island', according to the contemporary journalist Henry Mayhew. At this time, the Port of London was still among the largest in the world, a centre of manufacturing and of the supply chain for the rest of the country. Vessels of all kinds including massive ocean-going coal ships like *Bywell Castle*, passenger steamers such as *Princess Alice* and small lighters and barges crowded the river, filled with cargo and people (fig. 4). Charles Dickens Jr.'s *Dickens's Dictionary of London* (1879) contained printed lists of stops, prices and timetables, hinting at how busy the river must have been with passenger steamers alone. Shorter trips, such as from London Bridge to Chelsea, ran every ten minutes from 9 a.m. to 7 p.m., while in the opposite direction boats left Westminster for Woolwich every half hour from 8.10 a.m. to 6.40 p.m. This was in addition to

FIG. 4
A busy scene of shipping on the Thames, William Lionel Wyllie, late 19th to early 20th century, drawing, 276 × 602 mm, PAF1248

the summer timetable of seven daily departures to Gravesend and four to Southend.

Traditionally, the movement of people across and along the river had been facilitated by watermen, essentially the taxi drivers of the Thames. Boats were rowed by individuals or groups and passengers would go down to sets of stairs along the riverbanks to call for a ride. However, in the early 1800s, the first commercial use of steamboat technology on the Thames transformed how people moved around the city, particularly to its outer reaches.

By the late 1870s, the London Steamboat Company was the principal operator of commuter and pleasure cruises up and down the Thames, with a fleet of around 70 vessels. It had been formed as recently as 1876 through the amalgamation of several smaller companies, including the Woolwich Steam Packet Company and the Watermen's Steam Packet Company. The merger was marked by the mutual exchange of identical wallets (fig. 5), each containing 50 guineas, presented to the new company directors, Lieutenant Colonel Addison and William Beckwith Towse Esq. The latter was the father of William Wrench Towse, manager of the London Steamboat Company at the time of the *Princess Alice* disaster, who would lose his wife, mother-in-law and four of his eight children in the tragedy.

FIG. 5 Leather wallet with inscribed silver plate, Mappin & Webb, George, Henry and Josiah Jones, 1875, 20 × 105 × 80 mm, REL0715

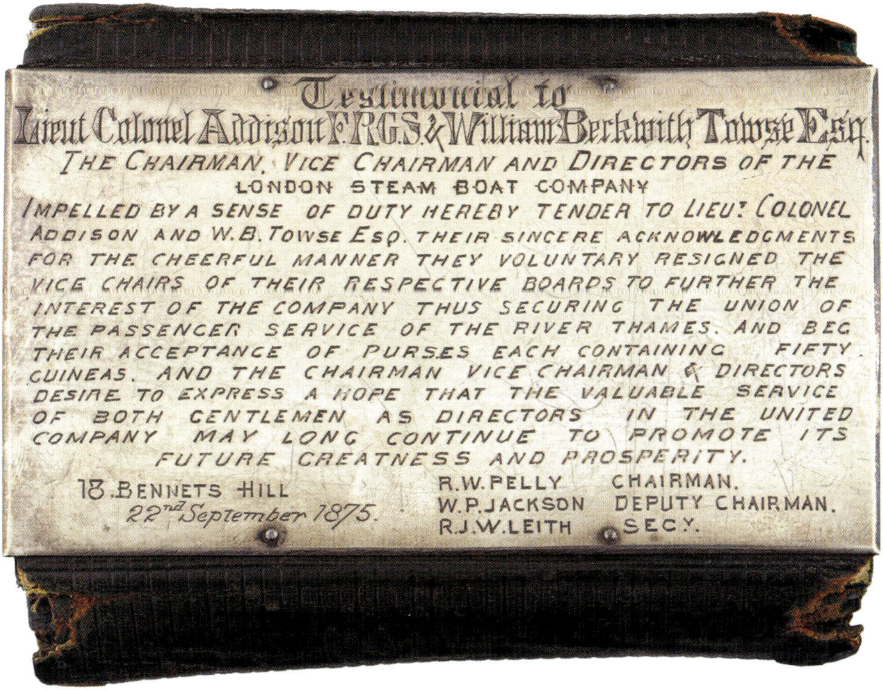
Testimonial to
Lieut Colonel Addison F.R.G.S. & William Beckwith Towse Esq.
THE CHAIRMAN, VICE CHAIRMAN AND DIRECTORS OF THE
LONDON STEAM BOAT COMPANY
IMPELLED BY A SENSE OF DUTY HEREBY TENDER TO LIEUT. COLONEL ADDISON AND W.B.TOWSE ESQ. THEIR SINCERE ACKNOWLEDGMENTS FOR THE CHEERFUL MANNER THEY VOLUNTARY RESIGNED THE VICE CHAIRS OF THEIR RESPECTIVE BOARDS TO FURTHER THE INTEREST OF THE COMPANY THUS SECURING THE UNION OF THE PASSENGER SERVICE OF THE RIVER THAMES. AND BEG THEIR ACCEPTANCE OF PURSES EACH CONTAINING FIFTY GUINEAS. AND THE CHAIRMAN VICE CHAIRMAN & DIRECTORS DESIRE TO EXPRESS A HOPE THAT THE VALUABLE SERVICE OF BOTH GENTLEMEN AS DIRECTORS IN THE UNITED COMPANY MAY LONG CONTINUE TO PROMOTE ITS FUTURE GREATNESS AND PROSPERITY.
18. BENNETS HILL
22nd September 1875.
R.W.PELLY CHAIRMAN.
W.P.JACKSON DEPUTY CHAIRMAN.
R.J.W.LEITH SECY.

Princess Alice, previously known as *Bute*, was built on the Clyde in Scotland in 1865 and originally carried passengers between Wemyss Bay on the Scottish mainland and Rothesay on the Isle of Bute. Both *Bute* and *Kyles*, of the same specifications, were bought by the Watermen's Steam Packet Company and renamed *Princess Alice* and *Albert Edward* respectively (figs 6 and 7). Lloyd's Register of 1878 describes *Princess Alice* as an iron ship, 219.4 ft (66.9 m) long, 20.2 ft (6.2 m) wide and 8.4 ft (2.6 m) deep. It was licensed to carry up to 936 passengers from London to Gravesend but only 486 to Sheerness as the river conditions were rougher.

Paddle steamers like *Princess Alice* were some of the earliest vessels powered by steam engines, typically fitted with paddle wheels on either side to drive motion. These were eventually superseded by propellers, which were more efficient and stable in open seas, but paddle steamers continued to operate on rivers, lakes and in ports, as they could navigate shallower waters and were easier to manoeuvre in tight spaces.

One of the first paddle steamer routes, established in 1815, ran between London and Gravesend. This route covered over 30 miles (48 km) and had previously been served by watermen. The advent of paddle steamers meant that longer journeys, such as trips from central London to the Kent coast or across the Channel, became much faster and cheaper. The General

FIG. 6 Paddle steamer *Princess Alice* (1865), unknown maker, 2006, 1:96 scale model, 290 × 713 × 123 mm, London Transport Museum

FIG. 7 Paddle steamer *Albert Edward* (sister ship of *Princess Alice*) at Cannon Street station from *The Thames* photograph album, unknown photographer, 1886, photograph, ALB0094

Steam Navigation Company, originally based at Deptford Creek, pioneered the commercial use of these vessels on the Thames, specialising in coastal resort trips in south-east England, connections to other British ports and crossings to France, Belgium and the Netherlands.

While earlier vessels were small and offered limited shelter for passengers, the rise of trains as a cheap and viable rival forced steamship companies to improve comforts for the one- to two-hour journey. They introduced multiple classes of travel, dining facilities and additional seating, including saloon cabins on the front and back decks and roof decks where passengers could enjoy the river's sights (figs 8 and 9). Catering crews served refreshments and live bands often performed on board, sometimes accompanied by singing passengers. By the 1870s, vessels operated by the London Steamboat Company and its competitors were larger and more luxurious. In 1878, at the London Steamboat Company's Annual General Meeting, it was reported that their vessels carried an average of 2 million passengers a year, indicating a continued strong appetite for pleasure cruises.

FIG. 8 Passengers on the aft deck of the excursion paddle steamer *Myleta* (1891), Edgar Tarry Adams, 27 July 1901, photograph, 82 × 107 mm, N19892

FIG. 9 'Departure from Greenwich. Scene on deck of Thames passenger vessel', Auguste Louis Lepère, 1891, aquatint, 225 × 287 mm, PAH3312

Day trippers and excursionists

While we do not know whether this specific ticket was used for the outward leg of the journey, many travellers boarded *Princess Alice* or one of the company's other steamers that September morning, setting out down the busy river either for work or to escape the city on an 'excursion', as these outings were known. Some passengers would have planned a longer trip, travelling down the Thames to reach riverside and coastal resorts that had grown increasingly popular with day trippers and the expanding class of holidaymakers in recent decades.

Excursions were advertised in newspapers and in purpose-made guides, with special promotions for tickets that included admission to attractions such as Rosherville Gardens (fig. 10). Extra departures were added to the timetable during peak seasons to accommodate the greater number of people travelling. These day trips became an increasingly important source of income for both the transport companies and the seaside towns they served.

The two-shilling fare advertised on Pa's ticket was less than one third of a day's wages for a skilled labourer at the time; children could usually travel for half fare, or for free if they were below a certain age. From the mid-1800s, rising living standards and wages, driven primarily by industrialisation, gave

FIG. 10 Advertisement for a steamboat trip to Rosherville Gardens, *The Hour*, 7 August 1876

FIG. 11 Holidaymakers on the beach and a sailing vessel in the water, looking towards Brighton Palace Pier, Francis Frith & Co, about 1902, photograph, G3032

., at the parish church,
ison, Captain 55th Regi-
nd daughter of the late
dras Army.
the parish church, Bexley.
'oodward Hooper, Esq., of
gest daughter of the late

d inst., at St. Ninian's
the Rev. George William
nts', Newton Stewart, to
Richard Jones Congreve,

d inst., at Dolphinton,
d son of John Marshall,
Susan, third daughter of
olphinton, Writer to the

ist., at St. John's Church,
rrow, fourth son of H. C.
Leeds, to Caroline, third
' Leamington and Hamp-

st., at St. Philip's, Alder-
vard, son of James Bloom-
and Manchester, to Lucy
ister Welsh, of Elm Bank,

t., at the residence of the
). Phillips, Esq., of No. 2,
eldest daughter of Lewis
quare.
the parish church, Broad-

OXFORD.—AT TWO EVERY SATURDAY.

CREMORNE. — BANK HOLIDAY FETE THIS DAY.—Open at 9 a.m. Fifteen hours constant amusement. The best entertainment in London. Monstre Programme. Three Bands. Dancing. Grand Ballet. Comic Opera. Acrobats. Gymnasts. Pantomime. Conjuror. Fireworks. Illuminations. Outdoor sports and games of all kinds. Admission up to 10 ONE SHILLING. After 10 TWO SHILLINGS.

Special Licence granted for MONDAY, August 14 (Mr. John Baum's Benefit). Open till 2.

BANK HOLIDAY.—THIS DAY.—ROSHERVILLE GARDENS, "The place to spend a happy day." —SPECIAL ARRANGEMENT with the LONDON STEAMBOAT COMPANY (LIMITED), the fares to Rosherville and back, INCLUDING ADMISSION to the GARDENS, will be only Two Shillings and Threepence. Ask for Garden Tickets.

RICHMOND and OXFORD via THAMES.— The ISIS will leave RICHMOND until end September every Monday 11.15; Windsor, Tuesday, 10.30 (train from Paddington 9.10) for READING, Henley, Oxford, &c. Ladies' cabin. Agent, W. R. Horncastle, 2, Queen-street, Cheapside.

BRIGHTON GRAND AQUARIUM.—BANK HOLIDAY.—Special attractions. Cheap excursions. Reduced admission.

Co.), and intend adding them to
SHOW ROOMS and FACTORIES
ING is completed; this Establishm
the largest in the World.

OETZMANN and CO.,
Extension of Premises, desi
for their kind indulgence under t
crowded Show Rooms, and other
the business having grown far be
which the premises afforded, notv
extensive additions which have fro
viously made.

TO AVOID the GREAT
men during the intended rebui
stock if retained, they have determin
the same at a GREAT REDUCTION
sell utterly regardless of their own i
must occur either by damage or re
alternative as most conducive to th
and seller.

MESSRS. OETZMANN
Patrons will avail themsel
they may rely upon effecting a gre
time, being anxious to clear out qu
fully advise as early a visit as con
selection. An Extra Staff has
prompt attention to Customers du
PER POST ENTRUSTED for
PROMPT and CAREFUL
KEEPERS and FAMILIES requir

more disposable income to a wider segment of the population. Working- and lower-middle-class people, such as clerks, shopkeepers, tradespeople, skilled factory workers and their families, increasingly had enough income to take a day trip or even to save for a longer holiday away from home (fig. 11).

The coastal and riverside locations, from Brighton to Margate, Scarborough to Blackpool, offered a welcome change of scene from dirty, smoggy industrial cities and the monotony of office, shop and factory work. They provided a variety of leisure activities and entertainments for visitors to have fun and relax. Some of these activities, like sea bathing, eating ice cream and taking walks in the sea air, had long been part of holidays for the upper classes. However, new attractions like pleasure piers sprang up, catering specifically to working-class tastes and budgets. These piers acted both as landing places for ships and boats and as entertainment hubs, with theatres and music halls, amusement arcades and stalls selling seaside food and souvenirs.

The increased accessibility of daytrips and holidays is reflected in the accounts and reports in the aftermath of the *Princess Alice* disaster, though these pleasure steamers were not required to keep passenger lists. While a first-class saloon was available on board, most passengers travelled on a standard ticket and the majority were women and children. Tuesday, 3 September

1878 was a working day and although occasional allowances of unpaid leave were becoming more common, those able to take a trip like this were usually engaged in unpaid, often domestic, work. Some children on board were in school-led groups, but those travelling with their families were either not yet of school age or on holidays from school, which had, at least informally, started to be provided by this time.

Excursions were frequently organised by groups such as Sunday schools or Bible classes, children's homes, employers and the increasingly popular temperance societies campaigning against alcohol consumption. Two Bible study groups, a girls' school and a children's home were all present on *Princess Alice* that day. Day trips to the coast were marketed directly to such groups, as they were considered a more acceptable leisure activity than the perceived 'traditional' workers' holiday activities like drinking in pubs, attending fairs or gambling at race meetings.

Beside the seaside

Rosherville Gardens, near Gravesend in Kent, was a popular day-trip destination from London. Built in 1837, it was the last of a 200-year tradition of pleasure gardens that had provided important leisure sites for London and its surrounding areas. For the affordable admission of a sixpence, visitors could

ROSHERVILLE.

"THE PLACE TO SPEND A HAPPY DAY."

R. CHILDS LITH.

J. HARDY IMP. 50½ HIGH HOLBORN

THE GREAT BURLESQUE SONG

ENT. STA. HALL.

WRITTEN BY

FRANK W. GREEN ESQ.

SUNG WITH GREAT APPLAUSE BY

JAMES HILLIER.

MUSIC BY

ALFRED LEE.

LONDON: C. SHEARD, 192, HIGH HOLBORN.

wander landscaped grounds dotted with tea rooms and bandstands, enjoying performances, curiosities and other assorted spectacles. Built into a chalk pit, Rosherville featured numerous attractions, including a maze, a bear pit, acrobatic performances and a lake. Visitors could also enjoy live music, dancing and fireworks, all promoted under the slogan: 'The place to spend a happy day.' (fig. 12)

If passengers chose to continue along the route, they would arrive at thriving Victorian seaside resorts such as Sheerness and Southend (fig. 13). Ornate piers had recently been built, partly as attractions but primarily to allow paddle steamers to land their passengers safely. Depending on budget and work allowances, Londoners might visit these resorts just for the day, stay for a week, or, in the case of the wealthiest, spend the whole summer. The first boat departing London on a Saturday morning was known as the 'husbands' boat', as men working in the city would catch it to join their families for the weekend.

The activities on offer in the late 1800s would not be so different from what we imagine for a British seaside holiday today. Sea-bathing was popular and was believed to be good for one's physical health. 'Bathing machines' – small changing rooms on wheels, pulled by horses into the water – were used to protect the modesty of female bathers. Holidaymakers spent time on the beach, collected shells, rode donkeys, watched

FIG. 12 *Rosherville, 'The Place to Spend a Happy Day.'*, Charles Sheard & Co, 19th century, cover of a collection of sheet music, Victoria & Albert Museum, London

FIG. 13 *Southend*, William Lionel Wyllie, about 1905, watercolour, 189 × 344 mm, PAF0853

Punch and Judy puppet shows, bought souvenirs and visited the pier (figs 14 and 15). One of the passengers caught up in the *Princess Alice* incident, William Bishop, remarked to a woman travelling with her three children that 'the water does the little folks so much good'.

At the end of the day, the tired holidaymakers, workers and day trippers would have gathered at the end of one of the piers awaiting the arrival of their return ship. On this fateful day,

FIG. 14 Holidaymakers and boats on the beach, with Brighton Palace Pier in the background, Francis Frith & Co, about 1902, photograph, 151 × 215 mm, G3031

Princess Alice began its return journey a little after 4 p.m. It was one of the last departures of the day, leaving Gravesend just before 6 p.m. and Rosherville Gardens at 6.30 p.m. By the time the steamer left Rosherville, it was carrying an estimated 800 passengers.

FIG. 15 Punch and Judy puppets, unknown maker, twentieth century, 445 × 310 × 100 mm and 710 × 320 × 100 mm, ZBA2300 and ZBA2308

Chapter 2

'Awful beyond anything I can describe'

The crew of *Princess Alice* was navigating back towards Woolwich and central London. The ship was busy; the fellow passenger William Bishop had spoken to remarked that if she had known 'so many people were coming on board I would have come back by train [...] I am always nervous when the boats get so crowded.' Bishop himself told the *Daily Chronicle* that he 'did not see a vacant seat anywhere'. However, the ship was carrying fewer people than its maximum capacity of 936. As night fell, some passengers had retreated to the saloon cabins for warmth and food, while others remained on the outside decks to enjoy the lights and fresh air. Singing filled the decks, both from the band and from smaller groups, as the boat meandered up the river towards home.

Meanwhile, in Millwall Docks, Captain Thomas Harrison (1834–1907), master of *Bywell Castle*, a ship double the size of *Princess Alice* at 250 ft (76.2 m) long and with a capacity of 892 tons, was preparing his empty vessel to return to Newcastle for its next cargo and was finally departing down the river towards the Thames Estuary. The ship had recently been in dry dock for repainting and its departure was further delayed by river traffic. Harrison had employed a Thames pilot, Thomas Dix, a highly trained captain who specialised in navigating the specific waters of rivers and ports. The Thames, with its constantly shifting sand and mud beds, notoriously challenging tides and currents and heavy traffic, required detailed knowledge and experience to navigate safely (fig. 16).

Princess Alice, now making its way upriver under the control of Captain Grinsted, was just rounding a bend in the Thames known as Tripcock Point, between modern-day Gallions Reach and Barking on the north side and Thamesmead on the south, near the eastern end of London City Airport today. At the time, the area was only sparsely dotted with small towns, many built to house workers employed at the Crossness and Abbey Mills sewage works and the Beckton Gasworks.

Accounts of what happened vary slightly, but at some point between 7 and 8 p.m., the singing was abruptly cut short. *Princess Alice*'s engineer Thomas Longhurst told the Board

FIG. 16
'River Thames, from London to Gravesend. Surveyed by Captain F. Bullock and Lieutenant E. Burstal, 1803–33', Hydrographic Office, 1871, 690 × 1,015 mm, G218:9/99

E S S E X
Proposed Canal or Docks
North Woolwich Railway
Victoria Docks
Plumstead Marshes
Erith Marshes
WOOLWICH
North Kent Railway
K E N T
E S S E X
London Tilbury and Southend Railway
Black Shelf
K E N T
GRAVESEND
North Kent Railway

2484

of Trade inquiry that he received the urgent commands to 'Ease her! Stop her!' A passenger named Mr Huddart told the inquest that he heard the captain shout, 'Where are you coming to? Good God! Where are you coming to?'

Moments later, the huge bow of *Bywell Castle* loomed above the passengers on board *Princess Alice* and ploughed right into the right-hand, or starboard, side (fig. 17). Longhurst was thrown across the engine room as *Bywell Castle* crushed *Princess Alice*'s engines. William Law, *Princess Alice's* second steward, relayed to *The Times* the chaos that followed: 'I ran upon deck, and amid the confusion and screams of the passengers I heard the water rushing in below and saw that we were sinking.'

Some passengers were thrown into the river by the force of the impact. Others tried to stay on board as long as possible but the front of *Princess Alice* tipped sharply, hurling even more passengers into the cold, dark water. *Bywell Castle*, undamaged by the collision, had crushed *Princess Alice*'s paddle box and engines and torn directly into the crowded saloon, flooding it so quickly that many passengers had no chance of escape. The river rapidly became a mass of drowning people. Survivor James Lynn described finding himself 'in the water with a lot of other people struggling and screaming'. An unnamed passenger quoted in *The Daily Telegraph* said: 'The shrieks and cries were awful beyond anything I can describe.'

FIG. 17 *The Loss of the 'Princess Alice' saloon steamer in the Thames, Sept 3rd, 1878. An Authentic Narrative by a Survivor, not hitherto published*, published by J. F. Nash, 1878, pamphlet, 252 × 190 mm, PAD6772

"Then rose from stream to sky a wild farewell,
Then shrieked the timid, and stood still the brave."

THE LOSS
OF THE
PRINCESS ALICE

SALOON STEAMER in the THAMES, Sept. 3rd, 1878.

AN AUTHENTIC NARRATIVE by a **SURVIVOR**, not hitherto published.

Heartrending Details—Facts not made Public—Noble Efforts to Save Life—Robbing the Dead—Particulars as to Lost, Saved, and Missing—Plan of the Locality.

SKETCHES BY AN EYE WITNESS.

BEAUTIFUL POEM, specially written on the event,
NOW FIRST PUBLISHED.

A MEMORIAL FOR ALL TIME OF THIS FEARFUL CALAMITY.

WHOLESALE OF J. F. NASH, 75, FLEET STREET, E.C.

Princess Alice was completely submerged within five minutes. The strong currents and tides of the river, and struggling victims all around, challenged even the strongest swimmers, though few people at the time would have been able to swim. Many survivors' accounts spoke of the confusion and terror in the water. Those who managed to swim to safety were primarily men, as they were more likely to have learnt to swim and were typically wearing lighter and less restrictive clothing. Claude Wiele, a clerk, and his brother Herbert, returning from three days' holiday at Sheerness, described jumping into the river after removing their boots, coats and waistcoats, then swimming to the safety of *Bywell Castle*. William Law recounted carrying his girlfriend on his shoulder and jumping overboard, confident he could swim to the shore. He lost hold of her and dove to look for her to no avail. He was able to grab another gentleman, Mr Talbot of Forest Hill, keeping him afloat until they were rescued. Another passenger, Inspector King of the Thames Police, who lost seven members of his family in the disaster, thought he had been able to rescue his wife, but on reaching safety found he had saved a different woman entirely.

Some passengers managed to cling to debris from the wreck or to ropes, buoys, life rings and broken-up supply boxes from *Bywell Castle*. Captain Harrison reported that his crew was 'saving life by throwing ropes overboard and hauling people up over the bows' and that he 'sang out to get out the starboard aft lifeboat'. They were soon assisted by surviving passengers from *Princess Alice*, people who had only just escaped the water themselves. *Princess Alice*'s cook, Mr Merriman, reported holding onto a rope for 20 minutes, with four men and women clinging in turn to his clothes before they were rescued. Henry Reed, a stationer who lived on Oxford Street, and his wife clung to a plank for over 3 km (2 miles) before they were picked up by a rowing boat and set ashore at Greenwich. Another paddle steamer, *Duke of Teck*, coming upriver just behind *Princess Alice*, was also able to take on board both survivors and bodies, particularly from the smaller rowing boats and lifeboats that were rapidly becoming overloaded.

The commotion on the river drew the attention of nearby residents, workers at the Lawes Manure Factory and Beckton Gasworks (fig. 18) and crews on surrounding barges and boats, many of whom rushed to rescue anyone they could reach. Bargemen from Beckton alone reportedly managed to save up to 40 people from the water. A number of rescuers were later formally acknowledged, including Sergeant Major A.J. Brown, who was awarded a medal (fig. 19), while many others were recognised in newspaper accounts published around the country. Joseph Smith, master of a nearby vessel, took out his rowing boat but was 'nearly swamped by the crowds'.

FIG. 18
A view of Beckton Gasworks from the Thames, William Lionel Wyllie, about 1900, watercolour, 355 × 508 mm, PAF1560

FIG. 19
Lifesaving award presented to Sergeant Major A.J. Brown 'for rendering gallant assistance' at the *Princess Alice* wreck, 1878, silver medal, diam. 32 mm, MED0586

PRESENTED
TO
FOR RENDERING
GALLANT ASSISTANCE
at the wreck of the

He managed to save 11 people before being forced to withdraw for fear his boat would be overwhelmed. Residents in nearby Woolwich and Creekmouth opened their homes to survivors, tending to their needs and sharing what clothes and food they had. As one newspaper observed, 'many of the inhabitants of Woolwich passed the whole night by the water side, in their anxiety to be of use'.

By the time news of the collision had spread and the authorities had fully grasped what had happened, the effort had shifted from rescue to the recovery and care of victims' bodies (fig. 20). No one had a clear idea of how many had been saved and how many were lost. Some survivors had gone home as soon as they were able, perhaps in shock. Others were scattered across three counties, housed variously in private homes, infirmaries and hospitals, government buildings, factories and the offices of the London Steamboat Company. Several places on both banks of the river had become makeshift morgues, from the steamboat company's office to Woolwich Town Hall and the Lawes factory in Creekmouth. A report in *The Times* on Thursday, 5 September described the streets of Woolwich as 'filled with people of all sexes and ages hurrying from point to point to seek the bodies of their friends, a very sorrowful and anxious crowd'.

While Woolwich Police attempted to manage the immediate aftermath, alongside crowds of worried relatives and onlookers

FIG. 20
'The Great Disaster on the Thames: Recovering Bodies from the Wreck of the *Princess Alice*', *The Illustrated London News*, 14 September 1878

FIG. 21
'The Great Disaster on the Thames: Relics of the Dead Exposed for Identification at Woolwich Dockyard', *The Illustrated London News*, 21 September 1878

who descended on the town as the news spread, it was not until inquests opened, primarily the one in Woolwich the next day, that a more organised response began to take shape. The county coroner of West Kent, Charles Carttar (1809–80), requested military assistance to establish a single location at Woolwich Dockyard for unidentified victims. From the following night, all bodies recovered from the south side of the river, within Kent's jurisdiction, were brought there, so families at least had one place to attend.

Woolwich Police then implemented a system for recording each victim's apparent sex and age, along with descriptions of their clothes and any personal effects. These items were stored in what the press called a 'black museum' (fig. 21). This spared relatives having to view every body in the hope of finding their loved one; if they recognised a person's belongings or clothing, they could be taken directly to that individual. Each person was then formally identified before the inquest jury and subsequently released to their family. Although the scale of this disaster was unprecedented, Carttar's experience as a coroner and with managing the aftermath of tragic deaths enabled him to impose some degree of coordination and order on the proceedings.

'Thousands of sightseers'

News of what had happened on the Thames spread rapidly across the country, primarily via telegraph. The story, often reproduced word-for-word from London papers, appeared in many regional newspapers, from the *Dundee Courier* to the *Royal Cornwall Gazette*, by the following day. Much of the coverage was inaccurate, particularly at first when the facts were unclear, and some reports were sensationalist, describing survivor and rescuer accounts as 'thrilling' or the public response as 'excitement', while providing lurid descriptions of the wreck and the morgues (fig. 22). *The Illustrated London News* even published images that, by modern standards, are quite graphic. This almost macabre approach was certainly common in the press and other popular literature at the time, notably in contemporary crime reporting. Newspapers were rapidly expanding and competing for audiences and, as with modern tabloids, the most explicit and dramatic stories drew the most readers.

The Woolwich foreshore quickly became a site of pilgrimage. Members of the public travelled to see the accident scene, even as remains were still being recovered from the river. While some were families seeking news of loved ones, many were merely drawn by grim curiosity. Watermen even advertised trips to see the wreck for one shilling. Later in the week, when parts

FIG. 22
'How They Found My Poor Girl', print from pamphlet *The Loss of the Princess Alice saloon steamer in the Thames Sept 3rd 1878*, PAD6773

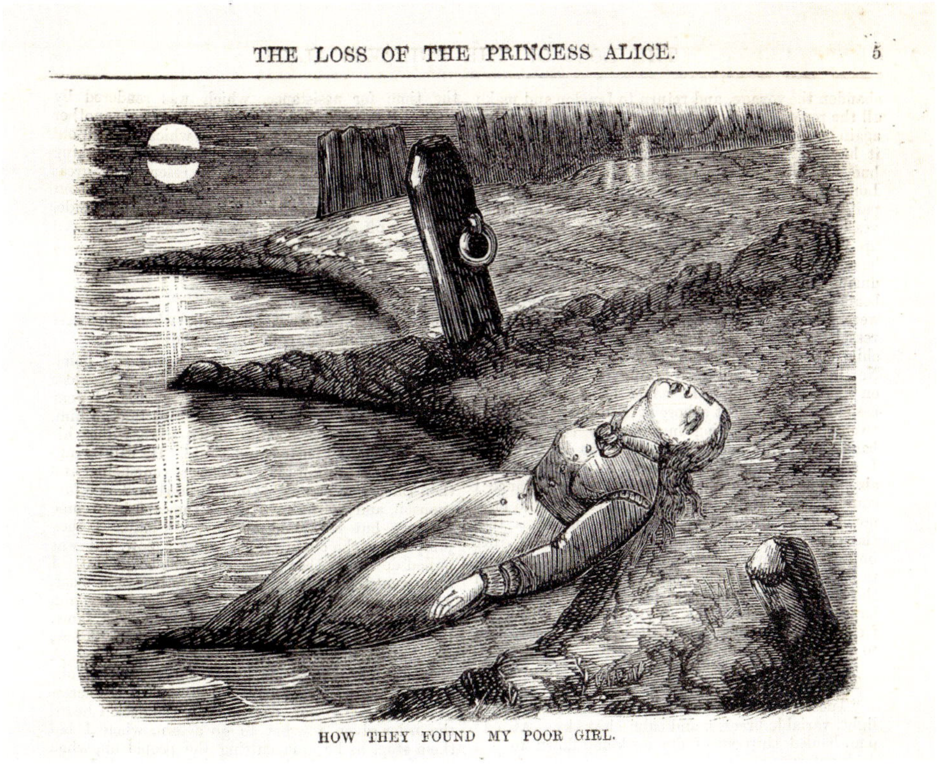
THE LOSS OF THE PRINCESS ALICE. 5

HOW THEY FOUND MY POOR GIRL.

Part of the Helm of the
Princess Alice Excursion
with the Bywell Castle off
Sepr 3rd 1878. 640 Lives lost

of the *Princess Alice* wreck were raised, the *Birmingham Post*, in its minute-by-minute account, reported that 'thousands of sightseers and grieving friends and relatives' came to Woolwich and 'lined the riverbank on both sides to stare at the wreck'. Some reportedly had to be stopped from taking pieces of the wreck, although the existence of Pa's wooden boat (fig. 1) and a handle from the ship's wheel (fig. 23) suggests that at least a few succeeded.

In a society in which mourning was often expressed through public rituals and material symbols, it is understandable that individuals sought to take keepsakes from a site of profound personal and collective grief. These tokens served as tangible, lasting reminders of the deceased, a practice deeply rooted in Victorian culture. The number of surviving relics of the accident implies that this was a common practice – very few, like the carved boat, would have held much monetary value at the time. The reason for keeping them, as for Pa, must have been personal. Perhaps the onlookers who took these keepsakes were participating in the practice of creating or purchasing *memento mori*, images or objects that served both as a memorial and a reminder of one's own mortality. For those for whom the trappings of contemporary mourning culture were often financially out of reach, such objects may have offered a way to express grief and to honour all those who died in the disaster.

FIG. 23 Handle of the wheel of *Princess Alice* with silver mount, unknown maker, 1906–07, wood, silver, 125 × 60 mm, REL0300

'Burial Monday'

The widespread public efforts to express grief and offer condolences following the losses on *Princess Alice* were also seen in public fundraising. The Lord Mayor of London opened the *Princess Alice* Relief Fund, which had collected £31,170 (equivalent to over £2 million today) by the end of September 1878. Queen Victoria and other royals contributed donations, collection boxes were placed across the country, fundraising performances were held by theatres and music halls and a report stated that subscriptions came from 'many thousands' of different organisations and individuals, representing 'all classes'. The Relief Fund received around 600 applications from those affected by the disaster. It provided financial support for widows, widowers and 310 other relatives left behind, supported orphanage or familial placements for 212 orphaned children and dispersed funds to nearly 60 survivors, likely those who were left unable to work by the disaster. The Committee of the Relief Fund had handed out £725 on the spot at the makeshift morgue, as some families could not afford the travel to Woolwich to identify their loved ones, let alone cope with the 'abject distress' caused by the loss of a breadwinner.

These funds could also help families cover the costs of burial. At this time, if the deceased's family could not afford a funeral, or no family could be identified, they would be given a 'pauper's burial', a state-funded interment, usually in a shared grave without a marker. Only the most basic elements of a funeral would be observed and such burials carried a strong social stigma in Victorian Britain, which people would go to great lengths to avoid. Many of the *Princess Alice* victims and their families were not well-off and were further impoverished by the disaster; without the Fund, they would likely have faced such a situation. That the Fund could be accessed specifically to cover funeral costs highlights how important it was to observe cultural expectations around death and mourning, perhaps especially in the context of a violent and shocking death. By helping to provide at least a 'proper' funeral, the Relief Fund may have assisted wider society in coming to terms with the tragedy.

The coroner expressed concern at the 'extraordinarily large' number of unidentified dead, and was reluctant to order their burials, fearing that doing so would prevent future identification and deny the deceased the rite of recognition in death with a permanent grave marker. However, due to the deterioration of the bodies, which were already damaged by the water and had remained at the dockyard for almost a week without refrigeration, it became necessary to proceed with funerals for those whose identity remained unknown.

FIG. 24

'The Great Disaster on the Thames: Burial of the Unknown Dead at the Woolwich Cemetery, East Wickham', *The Illustrated London News*, 21 September 1878

On what became known in the press as 'Burial Monday', 16 September 1878, the private funerals of 150 identified victims and two services for the unidentified took place (fig. 24). Once more, the public, especially the local community in Woolwich, went to great lengths to provide the deceased with funerals that met contemporary expectations. The unidentified were supplied with coffins by the local authorities, each fitted with a plaque displaying a registration number assigned by the police. This number corresponded to the victim's personal belongings, which were retained in the hope of enabling future identification.

There were two funeral processions, one in the morning and one in the evening, both led by mounted police. Local churchwardens were designated as chief mourners, leading the way. *The Illustrated London News* reported that the whole route was lined with mourners, with possibly as many as 7,000 attending at Woolwich Cemetery. A service was conducted by Reverend Anson, the Rector at Woolwich, and flowers were scattered at the graves by a member of the local congregation. Three coffins were reclaimed at the last minute by families who had recognised newspaper descriptions; these coffins were pulled from the processions and returned to the dockyard. A week later, the *Morning Advertiser* reported that the wreck, which had been moved to Plumstead, was 'visited by thousands' and that 'Woolwich Cemetery also attracted a large number of visitors, it being observed that some sympathising hands had scattered flowers on the graves of those who were lost'. Local communities and the wider public devoted both money and time to ensure that even the unidentified were mourned and given what would have been considered 'respectable' funerals.

The focus on ensuring appropriate burials and observing Victorian funerary customs is further reflected in the *Princess Alice* disaster mourning card (fig. 25). It reads: 'In Memory of Nearly Seven Hundred Passengers Who perished by the sinking of the Saloon Steamer, "Princess Alice," in the Thames, off Woolwich, September 3rd, 1878'. The background includes imagery of a wrecked vessel and a broken mast in the water, symbolising the tragedy. Mourning cards were a common feature of nineteenth-century funerary culture, functioning as mementos, notifications of death and invitations to funerals. They were decorative – printed, embossed and cut with stylised designs and symbols – and were often kept after the funeral as *memento mori*. The text on this example suggests that such cards were likely produced speculatively by local printers, or perhaps commissioned by a donor, to be sold or distributed to at least some attendees of the very public funerals for this disaster.

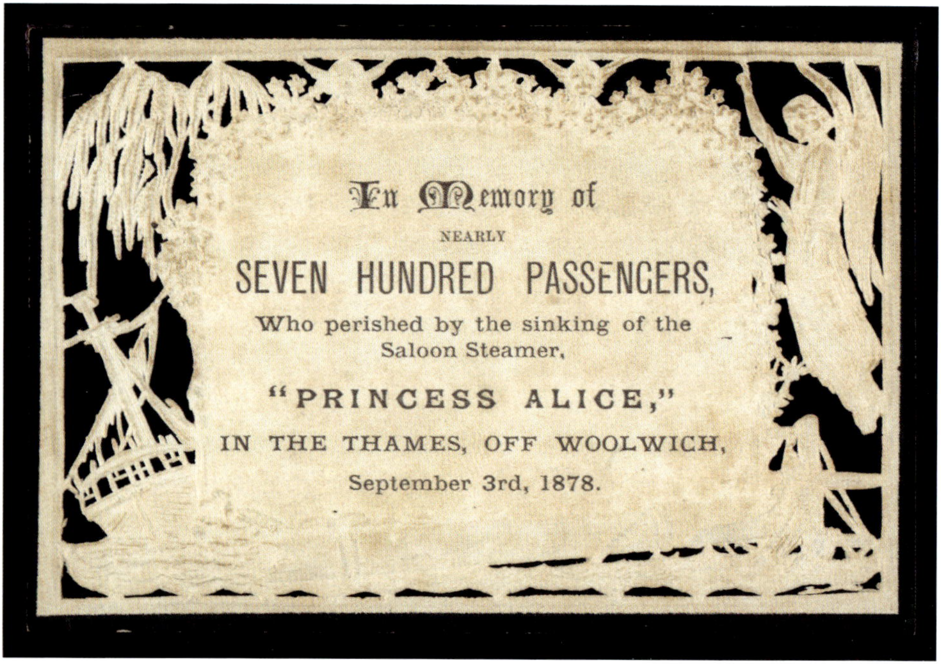

FIG. 25

Mourning card for *Princess Alice* victims, unknown maker, 1878, 117 × 78 mm, REL0778

The wrecking of *Princess Alice* in the Thames caused immediate and massive loss to the families of the estimated 650 victims, whose lives would never be the same again. Its impact also reverberated more widely across society. On an individual level, returning to the object at hand, Pa may have felt compelled to attend the raising of the vessel, taking his own memento of the near-miss that could have claimed his life and impacted his family. On a societal level, there was an immediate outpouring of public grief and attempts to ensure the victims received respectful treatment in death, regardless of their individual circumstances.

However, as often happens, the disaster starkly exposed society's hypocrisies. While great efforts were made to provide the unknown deceased with dignified funerals, it also highlighted the fact that many of these individuals might not have received the same treatment had they died under different circumstances. There existed a fine line between the genuine concern or mourning shown by some and the grim fascination or entertainment of others. Newspaper editors took advantage of this, keeping a rapt public hooked on the most graphic and sensationalist details and images to sell their papers. The aftermath of the disaster revealed both the most admirable and the more troubling characteristics of Victorian society.

In the immediate aftermath of the collision, multiple governmental and legal authorities sought to identify the victims and determine what had happened and why, hoping to prevent similar disasters in the future. Inquests for all the deceased were legally required to ascertain the cause of death and to examine the broader circumstances of the accident. In addition, the governmental Board of Trade, responsible for regulating shipping and investigating maritime accidents, soon launched an inquiry to determine the causes of the collision and whether additional regulations were needed.

Both investigations were completed within weeks of the accident and ultimately highlighted some of the most pressing issues in Victorian society: rapid technological change, the role and status of women, environmental conditions and wealth inequality.

The inquest and the inquiry

The official response came first in the form of an inquest, which was required by law in the case of any sudden, unexplained or suspicious death. This was led by the county coroner of West Kent, Charles Carttar. A jury of 19 men was formed, mostly of shopkeepers and tradespeople, who qualified to serve under Woolwich's property ownership requirements. Its aims were twofold: firstly to identify the deceased and establish the causes of death, and secondly to determine the cause of the incident itself, specifically which of the two vessels was at fault and whether the cause was accidental or the result of varying degrees of negligence.

The inquest opened the day after the collision on 4 September 1878. Initially, it was unclear how it would be conducted, as the deceased had been recovered or taken to multiple jurisdictions on both sides of the river. Normally, separate inquests would have been required. It was eventually agreed that each inquest would handle the identification of its own deceased and then adjourn until the primary case at Woolwich was decided. This approach avoided repeating evidence and witnesses and minimised the risk of conflicting conclusions. The juries also agreed to examine the cause of death of a single victim, William Beachy, with the understanding that their verdict would apply to all the deceased.

Carttar opened the inquest stating: 'All that could be done [...] was to alleviate the sufferings of the relatives by identifying as rapidly as possible the bodies of the deceased.' During the first week and a half, he took the jury to numerous locations to view the victims and the raising of the wreck onto the foreshore (figs 26 and 27) and hear evidence from anyone claiming a body. Witnesses were asked to explain how they had identified their loved ones and how the person had come to be on board. Once all who could had been identified, Carttar released the bodies for burial.

On Monday, 16 September 1878, the next part of the inquest began. Its purpose, in Carttar's words, was 'the important investigation as to the manner in which this lamentable collision, and still more lamentable loss of life, have occurred'. He began by expressing his displeasure that the litigation of events seemed to have begun already in the press by the respective companies and crews. The official log of *Bywell Castle* was

FIG. 26 Aft part of *Princess Alice* beached after the collision, unknown photographer, September 1878, photograph, P20979

FIG. 27
'The Great Disaster on the Thames: The Coroner's Jury Visiting the Wreck – Sketched from the Engine Room', *The Illustrated London News*, 21 September 1878

published by Captain Harrison and statements by crew of both vessels had been printed. There was clearly a lot at stake for both vessel owners and the surviving crews, and they were keen to influence public opinion. Newspapers capitalised further, publishing letters by a huge variety of 'experts', all giving their opinions as to who was at fault or suggesting inventive solutions and policy changes to avoid future incidents.

The inquest's role in ascertaining the cause of the accident also included deciding whether to recommend criminal charges. It examined a huge variety of potential factors that may have contributed to the collision. Accusations had been thrown at *Bywell Castle*'s crew and its conduct, including the Thames pilot Thomas Dix who commanded the vessel, and at the crew of *Princess Alice* for poor navigation, overcrowding and other failings. Legal representatives for *Bywell Castle*, *Princess Alice*'s London Steamboat Company, Dix and victims' families were all able to cross-examine those testifying. The jury was given a survey of the river, marked with the location of the collision, and models of both vessels to demonstrate their movements. These material prompts were designed to assist a lay jury in understanding sailors' jargon and descriptions of events.

The inquest heard from a very large number of witnesses: from the Superintendent of the London Steamboat Company, crewmembers of both vessels, watermen and sailors on the Thames that night, survivors from *Princess Alice* and a surveyor of the Thames Conservancy, the body responsible for managing the river and its navigation (fig. 28).

After some adjournments, a verdict was finally reached on 14 November 1878, two months after the inquest had opened. The jury apparently had some trouble coming to a unanimous decision and Carttar instructed that a majority would be acceptable. The long-awaited verdict was given with a majority of 15 out of 19; four jurors refused to sign it. It was reported in *Home News for India, China and the Colonies* as follows: 'They are of the opinion that the *Bywell Castle* did not take the necessary precautions of easing, stopping, and reversing her engines in time; and that the *Princess Alice* contributed to the collision by not stopping and going astern.'

The government response took the form of a Board of Trade inquiry, which assessed compliance with its regulations and whether any licensed individuals had breached them and were therefore culpable. Due to the overlapping remits, Carttar had hoped his inquest could be concluded first, so that the press coverage of each investigation would not affect the other. The Board of Trade, possibly eager to address speculation and rumours regarding the conduct of both crews and captains, pressed ahead and opened its inquiry on

FIG. 28
'The Great Disaster on the Thames: The Inquest at Woolwich Townhall', *The Illustrated London News*, 21 September 1878

THE GREAT DISASTER ON THE THAMES: THE INQUEST AT WOOLWICH TOWNHALL.

14 October 1878 at the Board of Trade court on East India Dock Road. The proceedings were presided over by John Balguy, the Thames magistrate, along with three naval assessors.

On 6 November 1878, shortly before Carttar's inquest concluded, the Board of Trade inquiry published its findings. It reached a conflicting conclusion, stating that 'the cause of the said casualty was the breach of rule 29 of the Thames Conservancy Regulations by *Princess Alice* not porting her helm when she came end on to the *Bywell Castle*, a vessel coming in the opposite direction...', which made the accident inevitable from *Bywell Castle*'s perspective. This perhaps reflected the difference in purpose of the two investigations. The Board of Trade focused narrowly on whether the actions of both captains complied with regulations, while Carttar's inquest considered more broadly whether any fault lay with either vessel and what wider factors might have contributed to the disaster.

Rules of the road

That the inquest and the inquiry could not agree on which vessel had broken the rules of the river underscores the point on which they did agree: that regulations for safely navigating the Thames, particularly for steam vessels, were inadequate and confusing. The Board of Trade report mentioned the apparent lack of awareness of and adherence to the existing rules of the river: 'It appears to the court that the error committed by the unfortunate captain of the *Princess Alice* [...] was entirely due to this irregular practice [passing vessels on either side when they met], no doubt, like numbers of others daily navigating the Thames, [he] was ignorant of any rules to the contrary.' The *Weekly Dispatch* explained, 'There are two systems, one not laid down by the law, but commonly recognised, and the other promulgated by authority, but practically unknown to those most concerned, it is merely a question of when big accidents occur.'

Steam vessels like *Princess Alice* were on average faster and larger than their sailed and rowed counterparts and thus could be more dangerous and required quicker responses from the masters and crew. In the November 1878 issue of *The Lifeboat: Journal of the Royal National Lifeboat Institution*, it was noted that, until this disaster, the rules for avoiding collisions in narrow rivers were the same as those for steamships at sea, despite the very different conditions. At this time, the Thames was growing ever busier, especially in the lower reaches east of London Bridge, as larger ships required deeper and wider waters. The day-to-day reality of navigating the river was changing faster than regulations could keep up, with devastating consequences (fig. 29).

FIG. 29
The paddle steamer 'Princess Alice' in collision with the steamship 'Bywell Castle', 3 September 1878, William Wilkins, after 1878, oil painting on cardboard, 214 × 346 mm, BHC3561

FIG. 30
House flag of the Thames Conservancy, E.W. Perrett Ltd, unknown date, 787 × 1,219 mm, AAA1023

In October 1878, before the inquiry and inquest had even concluded, the Board of Trade established an additional committee to examine the navigation of the Thames. Motivated by public criticism following the disaster, the committee's remit included:

> 'consider[ing] the rules now in force [...] and if any, what fresh regulations are necessary with a view to preventing collisions, and for regulating traffic [...] of the River Thames, bearing in mind the special points [...] the rule of the road, the lights to be carried, the use of signals, the speed of steamships, the necessity or otherwise of alteration in the regulations concerning the number of passengers carried by steamships in such waters, and as to appliances to be provided for lifesaving in cases of emergency, and the hours during which passengers should be carried in river steamers'.

It was also charged with determining 'with whom the responsibility now rests for making and carrying into effect the regulations'.

The committee, which became known as the Thames Traffic Committee, published its findings in July 1879. As recounted in *The Saturday Review of Politics, Literature, Science and Art*, it identified the 'enormous mass of traffic' on the river and the complexity arising from the wide range of vessels and their differing needs. It also highlighted that, in the absence of a single governing body, 'strange old rights' had been allowed to persist. At the time, five separate bodies, many represented on the committee, had jurisdiction over the river: the Thames Conservancy (fig. 30), Trinity House, the Company of Watermen and Lightermen, the Metropolitan Police and the Board of Trade. The report found that, although rules were in place, there was little knowledge of them or attempts at enforcement, as no single organisation held sufficient authority. As the committee concluded, 'that great catastrophe [the sinking of *Princess Alice*] made it clear that this state of things could not be permitted to continue'. It recommended granting the Thames Conservancy full power to regulate navigation on the Thames, giving one organisation responsibility for its management.

This ongoing debate eventually led to the establishment of the Port of London Authority (PLA) in 1908, creating a single body to oversee the port and the river from Teddington Lock to the North Sea (fig. 31). Initially, it held responsibility for the safe navigation of the river and was heavily involved in the creation and administration of new docks in east London, which helped to clear the river of much of its traffic and other obstacles. The PLA coordinated updates to technologies like dock cranes and railway lines, meeting the demands of a huge variety of vessels. The PLA still retains authority over navigation on the Thames today, although both the landscape and traffic have changed considerably.

The Thames Traffic Committee also recommended specific rule changes, such as how vessels should pass one another, the use of whistle signals to indicate turns, the display of additional lights on decks and on the port and starboard sides of vessels, and speed limits and restrictions on passenger steamers operating after dark. Foreshadowing the future moves of most London docks downriver into Essex and Kent, the report noted that the natural bends, currents, tides and sandbanks of the Thames, combined with the great variety of vessels, from passenger to cargo, made it difficult to implement consistent, simple rules without exceptions, as had been achieved in some more modern and accessible ports elsewhere in the country.

As with many government committees, its members were criticised for not going far enough in their recommendations. In September 1879, on the anniversary of *Princess Alice*'s wreck, a journalist for *The Times* wrote: 'It is natural to ask what steps have been taken to prevent the repetition of so bitter an experience; and it is disappointing to answer, "None whatsoever."' The article highlighted, even following the committee's report, that two recent collisions proved, 'that the *Princess Alice* was exceptional only in the magnitude of the ruin which followed the initial mistake'.

It is difficult to say how effective any of these regulations were. Accidents and collisions on the Thames continued and were treated, to a degree, as a natural consequence of shipping, a sector that, as *The Times* noted, contributed 'the most wealth to the port'. Technological changes in ships, the move away from commercial sailing and rowing, the increasing size of ships and the rise of other forms of transport – trains and later road – did eventually reduce traffic on the river, making it safer for the vessels that remained.

The next time river safety and navigation became a prominent concern in British society was in 1989, when a collision on the Thames between the passenger vessel *Marchioness* and the much larger dredger *Bowbelle* tragically claimed 51 lives. Echoing the events of the *Princess Alice* disaster, the eventual public inquiry, fought for by victims' families, identified many issues of regulation and safety on the river, ultimately providing 30 recommendations that ranged from vessel tracking to requiring historic vessels to meet the same health and safety standards as modern ships. The disaster also prompted the establishment of four Royal National Lifeboat Institution (RNLI) stations on the Thames for the first time in its history, with the Tower Bridge station now the busiest in the UK. Together, the two disasters serve as a reminder of the ongoing need for rigorous safety standards and regulation to protect those who travel on the river.

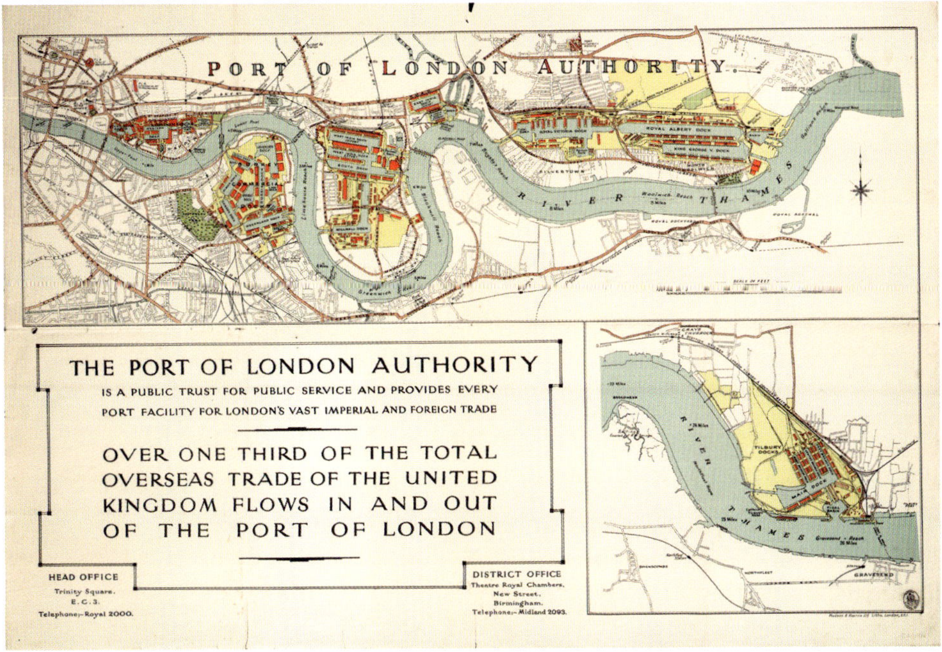

FIG. 31
Publicity poster for the
Port of London Authority,
Port of London Authority,
1950, 675 × 1,000 mm,
G218:9/6

Safety on board

The fate of *Princess Alice* drew attention to the precarious safety of Thames passenger vessels. In the addenda to its verdict, the inquest jury clarified that, while the vessel was seaworthy, it should have been required to carry adequate safety equipment for its size and that there were too many people on board that day, even if the numbers were likely within the permitted limits. River-based vessels had been largely overlooked in legislation – the quantity of lifebelts (figs 32 and 33) and lifeboats was not mandated unless they passed Gravesend and, even then, the requirements were vastly inadequate for a vessel licensed to carry over 900 passengers and crew. The Board of Trade concluded that the design of these passenger steamers had contributed to the disaster and therefore recommended relocating the lookout and steering wheel to a position above the passengers and in front of the funnels to improve visibility for the helmsman. Many similarly designed vessels were already in use on the Thames and on other rivers and lakes across the country.

However, this was an area in which the Thames Traffic Committee's recommendations were insufficient. Requiring additional lifeboats by law was ruled out as they would take up too much space on deck and require a larger crew to operate effectively. In the case of *Princess Alice*, the lifeboats had in

FIG. 32 Lifebelt from the paddle tug *Reliant* (1907), unknown maker, unknown date, 110 × 780 × 760 mm, ZBA4718

RELIANT
NEWCASTLE

fact been dragged down with the vessel. Life buoys and lifebelts were viewed similarly; they took too long to untie and deploy and were only really useful in cases where a single person had gone overboard. A vessel with 900 passengers could not carry enough of them to be remotely adequate in the event of a sinking. The committee therefore invited inventors to propose new designs that might improve the availability of flotation devices or offer alternative means of staying afloat during an accident. Proposals included floating seat cushions made of cork, already in use on similar vessels on the River Clyde. A man named Captain Warren suggested inflatable bladders that could be attached to men's hats or women's bags.

The committee ultimately avoided making any substantial recommendations. Its members concluded that the only practicable recommendation made to them was 'that the seats or other necessary furniture on deck should themselves be made moveable so that they will detach themselves if the ship sinks and buoyant so that they will float'. More generally, they suggested that efforts be made to design river steamers so that in the event of a collision, parts of the vessel would remain afloat and provide support for those in the water. All of these measures, however, involved significant financial outlay for the steamboat companies and the rebuilding of existing vessels and were therefore not made compulsory.

FIG. 33 Two studies of a seaman in a cork lifejacket, William Lionel Wyllie, late nineteenth to early twentieth century, watercolour, 353 × 251 mm, PAE3971

WHY DO NOT WOMEN SWIM?

A VOICE FROM MANY WATERS.

Ladies' National Association for the Diffusion of Sanitary Knowledge.

"Drowned, Drowned!"
HAMLET.

LONDON:
GROOMBRIDGE AND SONS, 5, PATERNOSTER ROW.

Price Two-pence.

Public perception deemed paddle steamers unsafe, damaging their reputation, and they never regained the popularity they had enjoyed before the disaster. It was not until 34 years later, after the sinking of the *Titanic* in 1912, that passenger ships were mandated to carry enough lifesaving equipment for all passengers and crew and, even then, those regulations did not apply to Thames vessels. Safety improvements proposed in the aftermath of the 1989 *Marchioness* disaster, requiring historic vessels to comply with modern safety standards and to carry sufficient life rafts and lifejackets, were not enacted until 2023.

'Why do not women swim?'

The disaster and its aftermath had repercussions beyond vessel safety. That so many people, the majority of them women and children, had drowned naturally triggered public debate around swimming abilities (fig. 34). Coroner Charles Carttar later noted, at another drowning inquest, that the *Princess Alice* disaster should have prompted everyone to learn to swim. Captain Matthew Webb, famous for being the first person to swim the English Channel in 1875, told *The Times*, 'because so few had taken the trouble to learn this movement, numbers perished within a couple of hundred yards of the shore'.

FIG. 34 *Why do not women swim? A voice from many waters*, Ladies' National Association for the Diffusion of Sanitary Knowledge, published by Groombridge and Sons, about 1865–85, Wellcome Collection

The reality was more complicated. Beyond the issue of heavy dresses, women were not allowed in male-only swimming pools and public facilities were scarce, meaning that anyone without substantial disposable income and free time was unlikely to attend. In the weeks following the disaster, newspapers across the country published letters advocating for improved swimming pool access. A reader writing to the *Fife Herald* argued that 'the value of this too much neglected part of education has been painfully illustrated by the late frightful steamboat collision on the Thames. Had all those on board the *Princess Alice* been able to swim it may safely be affirmed that very few lives would have been lost.' The *Sheerness Guardian* published a letter to the editor arguing that 'no one should be kept out by the price', and that the local baths in Sheerness should 'set apart a time each day for ladies and for children, and let them have family tickets at a small rate'.

Two years later, in 1880, *Princess Alice* was referenced to justify the need for new swimming baths in Tottenham, North London, pointing to the 'various baths which had been erected in the metropolis'. The disaster, the great losses and the notable survivals of those who could swim, had clearly stuck in the public consciousness and had, at the very least, provided motivation and justification for campaigns calling for swimming education and access (fig. 35).

FIG. 35
Swimming trophy won by Alfred Kneale, pupil at a Greenwich school, unknown maker, 1885, silver plate, 160 × 80 mm, PLT0264

‘Poisonous state of the water’

Swimming from the wreck of *Princess Alice* did not guarantee survival, as the polluted condition of the river posed a serious threat. The disgusting state and smell of the Thames around the site of the accident was noted by survivors, witnesses and those handling the deceased. Lawyer and sea captain Bedford Pim, representing a victim’s family at the inquest, repeatedly asked survivors whether they had consumed the water and what it smelled or tasted like. Most of those testifying remarked on the foul smell, with some describing the water as ‘slimy’ in texture. Unlike most of her fellow female passengers, Ella Hanbury could swim and survived the initial collision. She was rescued in Barking and returned to her home in Islington but ten days later, on 13 September, she succumbed to what her inquest called ‘congestion of the lungs and shock from immersion in the Thames’. Others had similar sicknesses following the accident and Pim used these incidents in his argument to the coroner that ‘death was due in many cases to the poisonous state of the water’. Science at the time was not advanced enough to understand the full impact of discharging untreated sewage into the river, so while it was acknowledged as a contributing factor to the losses of life, it was not officially recorded as a cause of death of any of the victims.

FIG. 36
'The London Bathing Season',
Punch Magazine, 18 June 1859

The 'Great Stink' that overwhelmed London just 20 years earlier – caused by the toxic mix of sewage and industrial run-off flowing directly into the River Thames and hot weather – prompted government action to fix the city's sewers (fig. 36). Joseph Bazalgette (1819–91), Chief Engineer of London's Metropolitan Board of Works, which was responsible for the city's public infrastructure, had designed a modern sewerage system to carry waste underground to treatment plants at Deptford, Abbey Mills, Crossness and Chelsea, before returning it to the river and out to sea. In 1870 the final part of this project was completed and it was touted by *The Guardian* as 'a wonder of the industrial world'.

FIG. 37 'Gallion's Reach looking south-west from entrance to Barking Creek (beside Lawes Chemical Manure Co Ltd)', James McBey, late nineteenth to early twentieth century, drawing, 262 × 728 mm, PAF5373

However, the testimony of *Princess Alice* survivors cast doubt on the scheme's effectiveness. Many had entered the water right next to the outlets from the Crossness and Abbey Mills pumping stations and found that the polluted water was not being adequately removed from the river at all, just deposited further downstream, away from the noses of the city-dwellers (fig. 37).

The evidence of the survivors and the condition of bodies recovered from the river did lead Bazalgette to reconsider the issue of sewage in the Thames. Members of the Metropolitan Board of Works, including Bazalgette himself, took samples along the river. *The Times* reported that 'at Victoria-docks [...] there was floating on the river much impurity' and that water taken from the bottom of the river, 'where the *Princess Alice* went down [...] was somewhat turbid in character'. They found that off Beckton Gasworks 'no fish life could exist in the water polluted by the mud in front of these works', and that under the outfall 'the mud taken was distinctly mixed with sewage matter'. While many factors were at play in polluting the Thames, the attention drawn to the issue by the *Princess Alice* disaster forced public bodies to acknowledge the problem and seek solutions. A decade later, Bazalgette finally came up with a solution: extracting solid waste from the sewage and carrying it out to sea, a practice that continued until the late 1990s.

The *Princess Alice* disaster, and the inquests and government inquiries that followed, put under the spotlight many social and political issues of contemporary society, bringing them to public attention and instigating campaigns for change, much as similar tragedies do today. It exposed the poverty, loneliness and vulnerability of many living in the city, the filth and overcrowding of the Thames caused by rapid urban expansion and the dangers posed by modern technologies when left inadequately regulated. The wide-ranging impacts of the disaster on British society were felt long after the tragedy itself had faded from collective memory.

Memento Mori

Despite being one of the deadliest maritime disasters in British history and certainly on the Thames, the *Princess Alice* disaster is little known today, even among Londoners. In contrast, the story of the *Titanic*, which sank 34 years later, has been immortalised in countless ways, while *Princess Alice* and its victims seemed to fade quickly from the public consciousness.

The *Princess Alice* disaster is commemorated by a memorial in Woolwich cemetery, where the unidentified victims were buried. A large Celtic-style cross was erected in 1880, after the Rector of Woolwich, Reverend Anson, who had overseen so many of the burials, raised funds through a sixpenny collection that drew contributions from 23,000 people nationwide. More recently, a small plaque on the north bank of the river near the site of the collision and a mural in Barking by Tamara Froud (fig. 38) also serve to remember the tragedy, either to preserve the memory of it, or to resurrect it. But why has a disaster that claimed over 600 lives and horrified Victorian society been largely forgotten?

Sadly, the answer likely lies in the ordinariness of the vessel, the passengers and the events themselves. *Princess Alice* was an everyday vessel, not luxurious, travelling down the dirty, busy Thames on a trip it made daily. Its passengers were

FIG. 38
Soul Searching in Creekmouth,
Tamara Froud, 2015, mosaic mural

mostly commuters and day trippers, largely working class, not wealthy or prominent in wider society. Their lives and experiences just did not attract the same level of public interest or eventual memorialisation as those of the rich and famous, particularly within the rigid class structures of Victorian Britain.

Despite this relative lack of public remembrance, the events of 3 September 1878 were certainly not forgotten by the individuals and their families directly affected. Many surviving objects relating to *Princess Alice* now found in museum collections like those at Royal Museums Greenwich, including a diorama model (fig. 39), are deeply personal reminders of the disaster and its impact. The diorama's maker, Henry Cartey, has carefully reconstructed the fateful moments and incorporated actual relics of the disaster: a damaged and discoloured pocket watch and another memorial card. Like the person who carved the wooden boat (fig. 1), Cartey was so affected by *Princess Alice* that he spent time making his own memento of the disaster.

In many ways, Pa's ticket and carved boat are as meaningful as grand public memorials. Though Pa's identity has been lost to history, the makeshift 'memorial' he and his family created through these objects has been preserved and passed down. Nearly 150 years later, it keeps the memory of the disaster and its victims alive and tangible, just as powerfully as any stone monument or plaque.

FIG. 39

Scenic model depicting the aftermath of the collision between *Princess Alice* and *Bywell Castle*, Henry Cartey, late nineteenth century, 292 x 654 × 407 mm, SLR2173

In Memory of
NEARLY
SEVEN HUNDRED PASSENGERS,
Who perished by the sinking of the
Saloon Steamer,
"PRINCESS ALICE,"
IN THE THAMES, OFF WOOLWICH,
September 3rd, 1878.

Further Reading

Flanders, Judith, *The Invention of Murder. How the Victorians Revelled in Death and Detection and Invented Modern Crime*, Harper Press, London, 2011

Gladwell, Andrew, *London's Pleasure Steamers*, Amberley Publishing, Stroud, 2015

Halliday, Stephen, *The Great Stink of London. Sir Joseph Bazalgette and the Cleansing of the Victorian Metropolis,* The History Press, Cheltenham, 1999

Lock, Joan, *The* Princess Alice *Disaster*, Robert Hale, London, 2013

Porter, Roy, *London: a social history*, Penguin, London, 2000

Strange, Julie-Marie, *Death, Grief and Poverty in Britain, 1870–1914*, Cambridge University Press, Cambridge, 2005

Thurston, Gavin, *The Great Thames Disaster*, George Allen & Unwin, London, 1965

Walton, John K., *The English Seaside Resort: A Social History*, 1750–1914, Leicester University Press, Leicester, 1983

Weightman, Gavin, *London River. The Thames Story*, Collins & Brown, London, 1990

White, Jerry, *London in the Nineteenth Century: 'A Human Awful Wonder of God'*, Jonathan Cape, London, 2007

Acknowledgements | Picture Credits

I would like to thank family, friends and colleagues at Royal Museums Greenwich who have listened to and supported me through the process of researching and writing this book. I would like to especially thank colleagues from the Brass Foundry, Prince Philip Maritime Collections Centre, Photo Studio, Caird Library and Archive and Publishing teams for their help and work on making this book possible.

Every attempt has been made to trace accurate ownership of copyrighted images in this book. Any errors or omissions will be corrected in subsequent editions provided notification is sent to the publisher. Unless otherwise stated, images are © National Maritime Museum, Greenwich, London.

p. 12 sourced from the British Newspaper Archive
p. 18 (top) © TfL from the London Transport Museum collection
p. 23 (top) sourced from the British Newspaper Archive
p. 26 © Victoria and Albert Museum, London
pp. 34–35 © Crown copyright. National Maritime Museum, Greenwich, London
p. 43 Mary Evans Picture Library
pp. 52–53 Mary Evans Picture Library
p. 75 © Crown copyright. National Maritime Museum, Greenwich, London
p. 80 *Why do not women swim?: a voice from many waters* / Ladies' National Association for the Diffusion of Sanitary Knowledge. Public Domain Mark. Source: Wellcome Collection
pp. 86-87 © Aberdeen City Council (McBey Collection). Photo: National Maritime Museum, Greenwich, London
p. 90 by kind permission of Tamara Froud. © Tamara Froud

First published in 2026 by the National Maritime Museum
Park Row, Greenwich, London, SE10 9NF

publishing@rmg.co.uk

ISBN: 978-1-917985-02-4

At the heart of the UNESCO World Heritage Site of Maritime Greenwich are the four world-class attractions of Royal Museums Greenwich – the National Maritime Museum, the Royal Observatory, the Queen's House and *Cutty Sark*.

rmg.co.uk

 A CIP catalogue record for this book is available from the British Library.

Design by Peter Dawson, Ronja Rønning, www.gradedesign.com
Printed and bound by Green Leaf Production, Slovenia

10 9 8 7 6 5 4 3 2 1

FSC www.fsc.org
MIX
Paper | Supporting responsible forestry
FSC® C105997